The Amway Idea

The Amway Idea

INSPIRING SUCCESS SECRETS FROM
ONE OF THE WORLD'S MOST
SUCCESSFUL COMPANIES!

BY RON BALL

PUBLISHER'S DISCLAIMER: All of the information in this book is based solely on the opinion of the author – not Alliance Publishing, Inc. This book is not meant to be a substitute for seeking applicable counsel from lawyers, accountants and business consultants.

The actions you take based on "The Amway Idea" are strictly at your own risk and do not involve the opinions or counsel of Alliance Publishing, Inc.

The Amway Idea
Copyright ©2010 Ron Ball
All Rights Reserved

This edition published by Alliance Publishing Group, Inc.

For more information:

Alliance Publishing Group
3 Grant Square #360
Hinsdale, IL 60521

Published in the United States of America. No part of this book may be used or reproduced in any manner whatsoever without the written permission of the publisher.
ISBN 978-0-9787851-9-2
Manufactured in the United States of America

*To Amy, who first inspired me to understand Amway.
You are the most positive person I have ever known.
Thank you for everything. I love you.*

Table of Contents

About the Author	7
Foreword	8
Introducing "The Amway Idea"	10
1. The Beginning of the Dream	13
2. The Roots of Success	17
3. Attitude is Everything	22
4. A World Opportunity	30
5. Living Leadership	36
6. Inspiration, Inc.	42
7. Free To Be You	49
8. Guilt-free Living	57
9. The Soul of Amway	62
10. More Than Money	66
11. This Is Your Moment	72

About the Author

Ron Ball is one of America's foremost public speakers. He's been speaking in front of packed crowds since the age of 15, presenting live business seminars to more than 8 million people in 21 countries. With 11 books on financial and life management to his name, he's also a prolific bestselling author with book sales topping nearly two million copies.

As president of the Ron Ball Group, Ron Ball is a recognized business turnaround expert, teaching aggressive problem-solving strategies to more than 12,500 business people. He's spoken his words of wisdom alongside such figures as Zig Ziglar, former President Ronald Reagan, John Wooden, Charles Stanley, John Maxwell and many others.

Over 10,000 business professionals have attended Ron Ball's seminars on problem-solving. Ron's unique jump-start techniques can help any business or person get going and growing from the very first day.

Ron Ball
The Ron Ball Group
381 Maple Ave.
Prestonsburg, KY 41653
1-606-226-2294
ron@ron-ball.com

Foreword

I grew up in Pennsylvania in a Mennonite-like family with 13 children. Early on, we learned the solid values of hard work, sharing, support and delayed gratification. I quickly grasped the importance of a consistently positive attitude. I first saw the *Amway* marketing plan at age 24. It looked great, but would it really work? I made a decision to trust the *Amway* opportunity. It was the best financial decision of my life. My first wife Fran, who died in 2003, was my beloved partner in the early years of growth and development. We both gave a full commitment to our business, and that commitment resulted in a better income and a better life. I surrounded myself with mentors from the world of *Amway*. We learned to give ourselves to the people who had chosen to do the business with us. We were motivated daily by the desire to help them succeed.

As in any business, we experienced starts and stops. Some months were better than others. But we persisted. We had not signed up to quit. We were always determined to gain our freedom. We had our share of critical, negative, people who tried to "steal our dream." But the more time we spent with our sincere, excited *Amway* friends, the more we knew that we wanted to build a future with them, and not risk losing it with negative people who didn't believe in us. By the time we had built a big enough organization to generate income, we had fallen in love with our people. The business became more than money. It became relationships, travel and great experiences with fun people we cared about. And we even made money.

The business really worked and continues to work today. I received my first check from *Amway* in March, 1984, and achieved what is now called the "Platinum Level" in August of that same year. I have lived entirely on my *Amway* income since 1988 and have never looked back. There is no need to.

All this brings me to why I agreed to write this forward. I have known Ron Ball for years. He has always understood the heartbeat of our business. No one has supported us with more genuine integrity. When I found out he was writing a book about *Amway Global*, I knew it was perfect timing. He has been a speaker, counselor and mentor to thousands of us. I have always trusted Ron to do the right thing. Throughout the process, Ron and I have frequently discussed and thought about the message of this book. I am touched at the good result.

Amway is not the same business I started in 26 years ago. It has become something new, fresh and original. *Amway* has changed into *Amway Global*, a better opportunity for this generation than when I first saw it. It is internet friendly, driven by exceptional health and beauty products. It is still led by rock-solid principles of free enterprise and personal, financial freedom. When Ron told me he wanted to call the book *The Amway Idea*, I knew it was winner, because it expresses that *Amway* is not just a business, it is an *idea,* a *belief,* and a *dream* that applies to anyone and everyone.

I know the *Amway* business. I built my business from literally nothing, to a "Diamond" level success. I know Ron Ball. He is honest, objective and thoroughly motivated to help the lives of people everywhere. I know this book. It may be your best introduction to the principles that created my success, and can create yours as well.

Happy Reading!
— Brett Deimler, *Amway Global Diamond*

INTRODUCING
"The Amway Idea"

"I want one thing. Can you help me change my life?"

When I received this question in the mail it rocked me. Here was a young woman asking for life-changing help. She wanted a red-hot answer to a core question. What does it take to get you on a success track? What really works? This book is an answer. It is based on my adventure with a business group that "wowed" me from the start. This business is the grandfather of all direct selling opportunities… **AMWAY**.

Amway is the pioneer of personal business ownership in the modern era. The principles and beliefs of its founders and leaders have built a base of success for millions of people, in every part of the developed world. Whether you are in *Amway*, will ever be in *Amway*, or know someone who is, these principles and beliefs have tremendous value for you. Anything that has generated billions of dollars for millions of people is worth knowing more about.

I did not discover *Amway* as an *Amway* business owner. My first encounter was as a guest speaker for an *Amway* event. I had already spoken to tens of thousands in conferences and conventions. I was unprepared for the level of enthusiasm and the deep hunger for excellence I experienced. The *Amway* people were different. The *Amway* event was different. The excitement was different. The quality was different. The underlying philosophy of success was different. I determined to discover the heart of this business that had such an extraordinary effect on so many individuals.

Introducing the "Amway Idea"

My speeches were very well received and I was invited to more conventions. I met and became close friends with Dexter Yager. I learned later that he had the single largest *Amway* business in the world. He introduced me to the *Amway* founders, Rich DeVos and Jay Van Andel. I met hundreds of remarkable leaders. I asked questions. I watched and listened. In time, my relationships opened doors that led me to understand what really made *Amway* work. That understanding is the foundation of this book.

Let me tell you a story that explains why I wrote *The Amway Idea*.

Tom is a 29 year old man working at an Audi dealership. He has an undergraduate degree in marketing. We met after I had given a motivational seminar connected to an *Amway* meeting. Tom was a super skeptic. He didn't trust me or *Amway*. He asked me why I, as a professional speaker, would attach my presentation to the *Amway* function. I countered by asking him why he had come to the event. Something changed at that moment. He looked down, and then lifted his head to look at me eye to eye. He said he had come because he wanted to find something that would make money and change his direction. He was embarrassed that he had not done more with his life. He had come looking for hope. (Remember the young woman I told you about in the beginning? This is the same motivation that filled her heart as well.) Tom decided to try *Amway*. Two years later, he told me it was the best decision of his young adult life. He said that what he had learned about life and success had escalated him to a higher level.

I know that you are looking for better financial opportunities. You want to pay your debts and have money to live your life any way you choose. You want personal freedom, unhindered by the drag of financial responsibilities. But isn't there more? I know

The Amway Idea

that *The Amway Idea* is the "more." The thinking behind this phenomenal success story is your key to "more." Something has influenced millions, and provided them with the desire and means to change their lives. Isn't it worth your time to find out what?

I have written what I call an "essence" book. I have simplified the *Amway* principles into an "essence" for each chapter. I have taken years of observation and research and turned that amazing information into the heart or "essence" of each *Amway* success principle. Here it is. Study this. Open your thinking. Prepare to learn. Get ready to penetrate into the soul of *The Amway Idea*. Discover how the principles that have led millions to exciting success and fulfillment can transform you today. Let the adventure begin.

CHAPTER 1
The Beginning of the Dream

The world is different because Gertrude Crowder wanted to help Helyne Victor. Gertrude was excited about a vitamin supplement that she believed had improved her own health. She knew that Helyne, attractive wife of the local milkman Joe Victor, had been confined to bed for several years because of rheumatic fever. Gertrude told Joe to give his wife the supplement, Nutrilite, and see what would happen. Joe agreed and watched Helyne recover and resume a normal life. The experience so impressed him that he decided to purchase the vitamin every month for $19.50 a box. He discovered that if he committed to 12 months, he would receive stamps each month that would create a discount the final 2 months. This is important because it shows that Joe was open to financial improvement. He liked a bargain. This led him to the decision to save even more money and become a Nutrilite distributor which would enable him to purchase the product wholesale, as well as sell it. Joe became a distributor under the sponsorship of Gertrude who would receive a percentage of Joe's revenue.

Fred Hansen was a well-liked barber in Michigan who had also discovered the health and financial possibilities of Nutrilite. He heard about Joe, a rising Nutrilite star in Akron, Ohio. Fred soon arranged to purchase Joe from Gertrude, who simply could not keep up with Joe's enthusiastic growth and increasingly large orders. Joe and Fred became friends and were joined in the business and friendship by Jere Dutt. Dutt proved to be not only

The Amway Idea

just as committed to the Nutrilite opportunity, but as full of integrity as Joe and Fred. The three established a relationship of trust and generosity.

Joe, Fred and Jere all moved up in Nutrilite and began attending motivational and training meetings called "Pow-Wows." Two other young men also attended and became friends with the first three.

These two were already close and had shown considerable ambition and drive. Rich DeVos was the son of a laborer who died young of heart disease, and Jay Van Andel was the son of a car salesman. Together they had sailed around much of the eastern hemisphere and tried numerous start-up businesses. They had a reputation for fearlessness and taking risks. The three friends and the two friends soon became five friends.

Joe, Fred and Jere experienced such success that they soon recognized the need to meet regularly for strategy and planning. These "board" meetings formed a forum for the discussion of principles they all agreed were critical to the continuation of their business growth.

Joe took notes and recorded what he later called the five pillars of their business. These pillars are sterling examples of the beliefs that are foundational to *Amway* today.

They include:

1. **Universality.** This is the belief that for a business opportunity to be good it must be for everyone. There are no exclusions and no exceptions.

2. **Repeatable.** This is the belief that a successful business should be based on selling products that need to be replaced regularly. The business model should be easy to

duplicate by anyone who chooses to do so. This implies that the people who present and pursue the business are trustworthy and have products and a business plan that will offer no negative surprises as new people become involved. Everything can be safely repeated.

3. **Unlimited.** To be worthy of the time and effort of an individual, the rewards of a business should be unlimited. You should be able to go as far as you choose to go

4. **Independent of any specific economy.** The business should be built on goods and services that are always in demand and not connected to the usual cycles of modern economies.

5. **Free Enterprise Driven.** This is the belief that human success is grounded in the God-given ability to pursue one's own dream of personal and financial freedom. Free Enterprise is the freedom to build your own enterprise for your own future. It is also the belief that as long as you pursue your goal in honesty and fairness, without harm to other people, you should be able to reach for your own horizon with no restrictions or interference, and the rewards you earn should belong to you.

This band of entrepreneurs soon decided that increased success needed an increased number of products. They heard of a liquid organic cleaning agent called "frisk" and arranged to buy it from its inventor. Their vision was growing with their sales volume.

On April 30, 1959, Joe, Fred, Jere, Rich and Jay met and formed a new way for them, and millions of others, to buy and sell goods and services. They called it the *American Way Association*. You know it today as *Amway*. Why the American Way? They had already agreed that this new way of doing business should be

The Amway Idea

universal and international. What they were doing was expressing the central theme of this book. It is the American Idea that is the basis for the *Amway Idea*. The American idea of personal freedom and opportunity is universal and international.

The five pillars that Joe Victor, Fred Hansen, Jere Dutt, Rich DeVos and Jay Van Andel committed themselves to in 1959 are the same pillars in place in the *Amway* of the 21st century. They are the basis of Amway's current and future success.

CHAPTER 2
The Roots of Success

In 146 B.C., the Roman general Scipio Africanus looked over the ruins of Carthage, the ancient enemy of Rome. An exhausting campaign of maneuver and assault had led to a crushing victory for the Roman legions. Scipio had master-minded the war in Africa and received the title "Africanus" as reward and recognition for his accomplishment.

But even at this high moment, the great general feared for the future of Rome. He detected the seeds of doubt, selfishness and indiscipline that would eventually destroy Roman greatness.

On a rise of high ground looking down on the remains of his ancient enemy, he spoke to an aide who recorded the words that made their way into the history books of that time. These were words, not about Carthage, but about Rome. Africanus saw the growing inner weakness of Rome and said that he already recognized "the smell of sunset."

This may seem an odd way to begin a chapter on the roots of the American idea of freedom, but any society or culture is capable of failure. When the reasons for greatness are forgotten, it is harder for each new generation to continue to enjoy the results produced by those reasons. The success momentum breaks down.

I was speaking at an *Amway* conference in Auckland, New Zealand. Auckland is a hilly city built on a series of extinct volcanoes overlooking one the world's finest harbors.

The Amway Idea

Earlier in the week I visited the berths holding magnificent private yachts from around the world. A dockworker pointed me to the largest and most impressive one. He had noted that I was an American, and said with the pride of inside knowledge, that this vessel was owned by an American. He waited a moment for dramatic effect, and then said it was owned by the famous businessman, Rich DeVos. This seemed appropriate as I was speaking at a conference for the business founded by Rich and his friend and partner Jay Van Andel.

My time in Auckland was filled with a fascinating collection of remarkable *Amway* people and memorable experiences. One afternoon I went for a walk to the top of a hill where statues of famous New Zealanders stood like silent sentinels in the wooded park. The University of Auckland adjoined the park. Hundreds of students moved purposefully between the park and the campus.

I stopped in front of a statue of a soldier. He stood in heroic pose. You could feel his courage, determination and sense of purpose. He represented the strong, clear-minded leaders who had protected the island and secured its prosperity. Then I noticed something else. His marble arm was broken. The sword had been removed and smashed. Someone had tried to carve graffiti vulgarities into the base beneath his feet. This noble defender had been attacked by the very descendents of those he had fought for.

This is an illustration of a murderous trend spreading through 21st century culture. A new generation has surfaced that still enjoys the residual rewards produced by men and women who understood the price for success. But large segments of that generation no longer follow the principles that gave them the security and prosperity they take for granted. They are like the empty-headed

The Roots of Success

vandals who deface monuments to the people who built their world. In both cases there is a fundamental disrespect for the causes of greatness. There is a core attitude of selfishness that blocks the development of the eight character traits that lead to successful societies.

The following eight character traits are basic for a strong, healthy culture:

1. **Work ethic.**
2. **Delayed gratification**
3. **A clear commitment to marriage and family**
4. **Honesty in all things**
5. **Fairness to everyone**
6. **Individual responsibility**
7. **Concern for the welfare of others**
8. **The pursuit of personal economic freedom**

We live in a "feel-good," therapeutic era. Many people quit when things become difficult. Many others choose to see themselves as victims who are treated unfairly by life. They believe that their experience would be so much better if only they could get the breaks they truly deserve.

In 1789 the faculty of Harvard University voted unanimously to "do their best" to teach the coming generation each of the following:

1. **Piety (a strong belief in God and a lifestyle that followed the moral principles of the Judeo-Christian Bible)**
2. **Justice**
3. **A sacred regard for truth**
4. **Love of their country**

The Amway Idea

5. Love of humanity
6. Sobriety (in a time of great public and private drunkenness)
7. Industry (consistent, productive work)
8. Frugality (wise use of resources and an intolerance of debt)
9. Universal benevolence (concern and generosity toward people in need)
10. Chastity (a positive commitment to sexual purity outside of marriage and sexual loyalty within marriage)
11. Moderation (a sensible, balanced approach to life)
12. Temperance (self-control and self-discipline)

They hoped that all of these character commitments bound together in the lives of their students and graduates, would be "the ornament of human society and the basis of a republican constitution."

When you study such a list you become aware that the American success story did not happen by some strange accident. There are specific roots that produced the fruits of the American idea.

What is needed now is a return to this way of seeing the world. I was first attracted to *Amway* not as a way to make money, but as a business that still believed and taught these "principles of greatness." I soon realized its capacity to provide financial opportunity. But the attraction of its traditional work and success attitude had already won me over.

I'm not saying that no one today works hard or that no one cares for other people. I am concerned however that the life principles that inspired people from other countries to come to America and build a prosperous society, are growing weaker. It is always easier in the beginning to let someone else, even the government, take care of you. But as time passes, you surrender more and more of your freedom. And as your freedom wanes, so does your independence and dignity. Strong people are self-reliant and secure. I suspect they are happier as well.

The Amway Idea

CHAPTER 3
Attitude is Everything

When I was 15 years old I asked my grandmother Lafferty why there was never any trash in her yard or on any other family's property. She said that caring for your property was the right thing to do. She was actually surprised, as if the idea of garbage strewn around was too silly to imagine.

This was in the 1960's before government welfare programs came to the Appalachian areas of eastern Kentucky where I grew up. I appreciate the help these programs have been to some people, but I also saw the way "welfare" sucked the soul out of many others. A culture of government dependency created a destruction of individual belief and effort. Even today, this undermines the dignity of thousands of people. Leaving trash in your yard is a symptom of a deeper problem. It reveals your character. Too many people have surrendered their humanity to bureaucratic systems that offer some benefits, but take away too many freedoms. This is why the *Amway Idea* appeals to me.

I was invited to lunch by a diamond IBO (*Independent Business Owner*) before I spoke at my first *Amway* event. After 15 minutes of casual talk, he leaned forward and asked what I thought of success. Did I believe in individual opportunity? What was my view of delayed gratification? I had discussed many topics with many people, but this line of questioning was new to me. I was impressed with the man's obvious sincerity, and gave honest answers. He smiled and said he thought we were going to get along very well. I learned from the start that the life perspective I learned from my parents and grandparents was completely compatible with the *Amway* approach to success.

This was reinforced one winter afternoon when I was having lunch with my friend Dr. Charles Stanley in Atlanta. I was giving him all the reasons I had recently come to believe that God would be happier with me if I chose to live in determined poverty and self-imposed obscurity. He sat up, stared at me, and stated that I had just proved that my God was too small. He exposed my false humility as a cover for my unwillingness to stick my neck out and risk the adventure of an honest pursuit of success. I was stunned by the direct assault on my hiding place and embarrassed by the accuracy of his comments.

My friend, billionaire businessman, Fred Wheba says that it is easy for pastors and other Christian leaders to become lazy because of the relative lack of accountability. They make their own schedules and hide behind barriers of apparent busyness. This is not a criticism of spiritual leaders in general. Many of these individuals live excellent lives of sacrificial service. But laziness and self-indulgence are traps that some fall into that stop them from being better than they are. My friend Fred truly loves Christian leaders and wants them to excel.

When Dr. Stanley confronted my lack of performance at that point in my life, he was pushing me into the open. He urged me to maximize myself for God's purposes.

This key conversation really helped me understand *Amway* – which was key for me when Jerry Meadows, a diamond IBO, introduced me to Dexter Yager a few months later.

My wife Amy and I were speaking for Jerry and Cherry Meadows in Huntsville, Alabama. The other speakers were Dexter and Birdie Yager. Dexter came to hear me speak at an afternoon leadership session. At the end, he introduced himself, and invited

The Amway Idea

Amy and me to visit him in Charlotte, North Carolina. Three months later we attended a large event with thousands in attendance. I listened to Dexter and other speakers describe the same road to success that my father and grandmother had shown me as a child.

This is a road to success that is marked by special road signs.

The first road sign is marked "Work Ethic."

My father taught me that work formed the basis of all success. Dr. Stanley, my spiritual mentor, said the same. So did *Amway*. *Amway* is not a "get-rich-quick" scheme. You are told in the beginning that your rewards are built on what you do – not what you hope for. This is essential to the American idea as well. America is called "the land of opportunity." It is for those willing to work for that opportunity. I once helped Fred Wheba develop a church at Beverly Hills high school in Beverly Hills, California. Early every Sunday morning, hours before our church service was scheduled to start, Fred, the billionaire, would arrive at the school to organize chairs and clean the auditorium. His work ethic is an extension of his character. I find that same commitment to hard work at the core of the *Amway* opportunity. You are rewarded for what you actually do.

Amy and I were having lunch at a restaurant in Lexington, Kentucky when my cellular phone rang. It was Rich DeVos, co-founder of *Amway*. He called to ask about my current direction. I explained my desire to use the media to reach more people. He listened and said he would call back with some ideas. Four weeks later he called again and gave me some excellent ideas to help me move forward. When he finished, he said something profound. He said that all the good ideas in the world are useless unless I was willing to seize them and work at them. This illustrates why I believe in *The Amway Idea*. Hard work is always front and center.

A second road sign is the concept of delayed gratification.

I write a weekly column at ronball.com called *Ballpoints*. One of my most popular articles discussed the power of your will to control your emotions. I told the story of Kayla and Mike, who in a flush of excitement, made a decision to build an *Amway* business. They found that it was not as easy as they expected. They came to me distressed. They no longer "felt right' about the business. They were ready to give up on a workable opportunity because their emotions were not cooperating. They wanted immediate gratification.

Jillian Strauss recently published a book based on two years of interviews that she conducted with young men and women in their 20s and 30s. In her 20's herself, Jillian wanted to create a profile of her generation. The results surprised her. Most of the interviewees had a "why suffer" mentality. They were weak when it came to any type of commitment, and frequently failed to show up for events they promised to attend. They refused to have a "settle for" approach to life and were willing to throw away responsibilities and relationships if they did not quickly work out. Their divorce rate was significantly higher than the U.S. national average. There was one thing they were sure about…delayed gratification was not for them.

This attitude is deadly to real success.

How can you do great things if you lack the discipline to "stay the course?" "Staying the course" is a key to reaching your destination.

You may know the story of the marshmallow experiment. This is a famous study of motivation.

The Amway Idea

A group of four-year olds was offered a choice of one marshmallow now or two if they would wait a short time. The majority chose the one marshmallow now (no surprise). But the most intriguing result occurred several years later. The study tracked those who chose (at 4 years of age!) to wait for the two marshmallows. The Stanford University study followed the marshmallow kids until 1985, when they were high school seniors. Those who had chosen to wait for the two marshmallows had higher grades, were much better at handing stress and had SAT test scores that were 210 points higher (on average) than the one-marshmallow kids. The delayed gratification test was a better predictor of success than their IQ exams.

There was a time in the United States when this disciplined approach to life was accepted and practiced. It was close to being a universal belief. However, in recent decades, most people have become consumed with the need to always feel good. They are impatient when results do not come instantly or even quickly. Their motivation to succeed doesn't survive when the reality of long-term commitment hits.

As I write this, my parents are preparing for their 60th wedding anniversary. They have lived a life of highs and lows; struggles and successes; victories and defeats. They have a rich history and hundreds of thousands of shared, hard-earned memories. They have managed their money so well that they have no financial pressures whatsoever. They are comfortable with their relationship with God and each other. They are immensely enjoying the mutual sunset of their lives. All of this is a result of several factors. But one of them is definitely "delayed gratification."

One reason I was attracted to *Amway* was their effort to restore this classic component of success to 20th and 21st century thinking. You can see why we need this approach again.

The third road sign is a consistent, positive attitude.

My daughter Allison, now an attorney, and Jonathan, an accelerating teenager, have grown up surrounded by the *Amway* business. They have absorbed the lessons of achievement taught by diamonds and other leaders. The best lesson they've learned is that you will go nowhere unless your attitude is always positive.

When Allison was nine years old, she started a positive pencil business. She designed and sold pencils with positive slogans printed on them. Her bestseller said, "Attitude Is Everything." She learned that from the *Amway* business. She no longer sells pencils. She sold the business to her brother when she entered law school. One of his bestsellers is still "Attitude Is Everything." He learned that from the business as well.

Why is a positive attitude so important?

Think of the car you drive. How far would you get without oil in your engine? You would soon be broken down and quickly stranded. A consistent positive attitude is the oil that makes the machinery of your life run smooth. Friction is unavoidable. The oil of your attitude eliminates the friction and propels you forward.

I was once with an *Amway* diamond in the wilds of western Germany. We were both scheduled to speak at a rally in a charming medieval town. Over a thousand people were waiting for our arrival. Everyone packed into the town's largest hall. We stopped at a nearby village for a quick meal. As we finished hot plates of wiener schnitzel and hearty German brown bread, there was an accident. A bowl of gravy spilled on the diamond's tie. He tried to clean it without success, then flung it off and said he would do the meeting without it. This mattered because the

The Amway Idea

German people are formal and have a strict business dress code. When I asked about this dress code, the diamond laughed and said that the meeting would be so great that no one would care how he looked.

Next, we drove to the venue and parked in the back. The diamond opened the trunk to get his dress shoes. He was wearing tennis shoes with his (tieless) suit and wanted to change. He rummaged through the trunk for a few moments and told me that his shoes were missing. Can you picture this scene? The diamond was preparing to speak to 1000 strict, formal Germans, in a dark blue suit without a tie and wearing glaring white tennis shoes. The audience was filled with attendees who had never seen the *Amway* presentation and were not persuaded about the *Amway* opportunity.

I watched this diamond-level leader walk onto the stage with confidence. He radiated a happy, positive attitude. I listened to him give one of the most effective marketing plans I had ever heard.

When he finished, the reserved German crowd gave him a wild standing ovation. My motivational speech was easy after this man's show of attitude electrified the assembly.

Hundreds of people signed up in his business that night.

Do you see why a positive attitude matters? He could not control the crazy things that happened before the meeting. All he could control was his attitude.

You can complain and bewail your circumstances. That is your choice. You can fly into a rage at the unfairness of your situation or relationships. But what good does that do? What will it change?

When you choose a positive response *every time,* you create the possibility of a positive outcome.

It's true…

Attitude is everything!

The Amway Idea

CHAPTER 4
A World Opportunity

I used to sit on the front porch of my Eastern Kentucky home and imagine all the places I wanted to visit. Our white wood home sat on a street overlooking the Big Sandy River. Behind the river was a mountain peak, green and lush in summer, white in winter, and a dazzle of color in spring and fall. The places I pictured in my mind had been discovered in books. This was my main introduction to the world outside Floyd County. Curiosity ran deep in my family. My Dad had left home at 17. He lied about his age and joined the navy. Since this was during World War II (and I know My Dad), I'm sure part of his reason was patriotism, as well as curiosity. My grandmother Ball was considered a legendary traveler in our town. I remember her chartering a private plane in her 70's so she could finally visit Wisconsin Dells.

Amway opened opportunities to travel that exceeded all my previous expectations. I have spoken at *Amway* events in Canada, Mexico, Venezuela, Haiti, The Dominican Republic, The United Kingdom, Holland, Belgium, France, Germany, Switzerland, Greece, Poland, The Czech Republic, Ukraine, Korea, South Africa, Australia, New Zealand and of course throughout the United States. I have been blessed with the itinerary of a lifetime.

The Amway Idea has inspired people in every part of the world. The business has improved the lives of men and women of every nationality and ethnicity. Color, place and origin are irrelevant to this mind-expanding opportunity.

I met a 27-year old man while speaking at an *Amway* conference in Johannesburg, South Africa. He studied to be a church pastor, and had to stop his studies to stabilize his finances. He was tall and athletic, with a warm, outgoing personality. He told me that he did not have any hope for a financial breakthrough until the conference. He had the intelligence and desire to succeed, but had not found a business vehicle that could carry him to his destination. When I returned home I received an e-mail from him. He had already started building his own business. You could feel the excitement, even through cyberspace. What he needed was a workable opportunity and he found it in *Amway*.

I was sitting in the kitchen of a home in Athens, Greece. Luke and Daniella are leaders of their *Amway* group. They met and married in the business. Their children slept as we enjoyed wonderful salads with fresh squeezed olive oil and feta cheese from a local village. We talked into the night about what they had learned in the business. They were amazed at the principles of free enterprise. Principles they had not known as they grew up. Luke would shake his head from side to side and speak about where they might have been if they had not found the *Amway* business. Daniella stood behind her husband with her arms around him, speaking about what Luke had learned in the business, regarding work, character and freedom, as well as how it changed him spiritually and strengthened their marriage.

They have developed their business to a level that has made a notable difference in their lifestyle. They have gratitude for the personal and financial benefits produced from their *Amway* business.

My wife Amy and daughter Allison went with me to Seoul, Korea. The city, filled with millions of residents, offered novel experiences. We were eager for our first taste of Asia.

The shopping was extraordinary. We were escorted to markets

The Amway Idea

where clothes were made for the great department stores of New York, London, Paris and Rome. We purchased this clothing for a small fraction of its retail value in other parts of the world. We were not buying look-alikes and imitations. We were buying the actual brand items. It was a shopper's paradise. The food was rich and varied. We ate Korean barbecue and sampled numerous versions of Kimchee, a blistering hot (to our palates) vegetable dish that is considered a national delicacy.

We visited shrines, temples and ruins that were up to 1500 years old. We also toured national monuments that swarmed with people.

All this was fascinating and enjoyable. But the crowning moment of the trip was standing on a stage in an auditorium filled with 12,000 Korean *Amway* IBO's. The crowd was respectful, eager, and above all, excited. When I finished I was met by hundreds of Koreans. Person after person thanked me for bringing hope. They were in the *Amway* business because they believed that *Amway* gave them an entrance into a greater life. Back at the hotel, I met a medical doctor who had built his *Amway* business to the diamond level, a significant achievement. He bowed graciously and asked what he could do for me. He said he wanted to express his gratitude for the business that helped generate his success.

I was ordering food at Heathrow airport in the United Kingdom, when my face appeared on the restaurant's TV screen. A news program was reporting on an *Amway* event and filmed me while I was speaking. I was pleased, but a little embarrassed. My mind quickly returned to the event itself. My happiest memory was standing in a line for two and a half hours while over a thousand *Amway* IBO's filed through to thank me for inspiring them to do their business. One couple from Nottingham could barely contain their emotions. They explained that their *Amway* experience had shown them that although they had started in humble, limited circumstances, they were not trapped. They could break out and be special.

I spoke to a small, new *Amway* group in Geneva, Switzerland. Men and women had driven from Western Europe to attend. They had finished work on Friday and traveled through the night to arrive on Saturday morning. I spoke twice that day and then stayed in the evening to hear their stories. One couple from Belgium had always thought that their jobs at a local insurance company were their one chance for financial security. They spoke in hushed voices of how an introduction to the *Amway* opportunity had blown apart their small image of themselves and what was possible for them. I had often heard the legendary *Amway* leader Dexter Yager tell people to pursue their dreams. Here was a couple who were living that pursuit.

I was speaking in Warsaw, Poland one spectacular June weekend. I was escorted on a tour of the old city by a couple who had been in the business for four years. I think they were selected to help me, at least partially, because they spoke good English. They were proud of their city and their history. We finished the tour at an aristocratic estate. We walked through gardens that were new when Napoleon invaded the city. Black and white swans, the traditional bird of royalty, drifted on the lakes and ponds that surrounded the white porticoed residence. We paused on a patio half the size of an American football field. Visitors in small swan-shaped boats shuttled around the largest lake at the base of the patio. I listened as a young woman remarked about her childhood under communism. She mentioned the forced uniformity of schools and the continual fear of the government. You were born in a certain position and you usually stayed in that position. Now she was in her 20s and faced a new life. She shared

The Amway Idea

how her mind had awakened to a belief that she could experience a high level of success herself. Her commitment to build the *Amway* business had raised her to a new awareness when it came to what's possible for her.

I was speaking to a convention of Mexican IBO's in Puerta Villardo. On Sunday after an interdenominational voluntary church service, I was surrounded by intelligent, motivated Spanish speaking *Amway* IBO's who wanted to talk for hours about their business opportunity. They recognized *Amway* as the vehicle they were looking for.

I had just finished speaking to a packed auditorium in Sydney, Australia. We were staying in a luxury hotel overlooking the Sydney opera house. Our suite was recently used by Queen Elizabeth II. The day had been spent touring Sydney harbor and the world-famous Tauranga zoo. We had played with kangaroos, petted koala bears and eaten under eucalyptus trees filled with kookaburras. In the evening I spoke to 5,000 *Amway* IBOs who roared their enthusiasm. When I left the stage I exited the building for a moment of fresh air. An angry man confronted me. He did not like a reference I had made about free enterprise. He thought I was pushing an American business onto his fellow Australians. I had just begun to answer him when an *Amway* IBO appeared. He had been listening, and assured the man that this business may have started in America, but was an Australian business. He described how his life had improved because of the free enterprise principles of the business and how the money he was making fueled his family. He emphasized that the success ideas he had learned in the business were universal and worked as well in Australia as anywhere else.

Two mornings later I was outside taking a break after speaking, when I saw the same man approaching. This time there was a dramatic difference. He told me how he'd gone back to the meeting and continued to listen. He opened his mind and saw the business in a new way. He apologized for his rudeness and said he had decided to do the business. When I asked him why he was previously negative, he said the problem was in him. He wasn't doing well with his life and wanted to blame something. So, he decided to blame *Amway*. He was sorry and expressed the need to do something that would get his life on a positive track. He even said that he didn't mind my belief in God, as he too believes.

I could continue with dozens of stories from more countries, but I think you get the point. *The Amway Idea* can and does work anywhere. Just as the American idea can and does work anywhere. People everywhere want personal freedom, individual opportunity and a way to succeed in their own business. I can say from experience that *Amway* gives them all of those things.

I want to share a memorable story that illustrates the universal appeal of free enterprise.

P.J. O'Rourke is a writer who has been published in journals as different as *The Wall Street Journal* and *Rolling Stone Magazine*. He was with the Desert Storm troops from the first Gulf War as they entered Kuwait City. The Kuwaiti citizens were delirious with joy at the sight of the soldiers. O'Rourke writes that a young man came running to meet them as they entered the city. The man recognized O'Rourke as a reporter and said, "We would like to thank every man in the allied forces. Until 100 years we cannot thank them. What they do is…is…is AMERICA!!!"

What *Amway* is offering is not an American-owned business that sucks the identity out of people from other countries. It's a business that represents the American idea. It's a business that in the true sense is AMERICA.

The Amway Idea

CHAPTER 5
Living Leadership

I first met Doug DeVos at the restaurant of the Metropole hotel in London. He was warm, open and made me feel important, as if what I said mattered. I was already familiar with stories of Rich DeVos, his famous father, and the company that Rich and Jay Van Andel co-founded… *Amway*. When I met Doug, *Amway* was huge and highly influential. I was in London to speak to thousands of excited *Amway* IBOs (although the IBO acronym had not been invented yet). Doug was there to greet them on behalf of *Amway*.

I had worked for five years with Dr. Charles Stanley, pastor of the historic First Baptist Church in Atlanta, Georgia. I had met many well-known leaders. I had always been curious about men of consequence and was eager to get to know Doug better. He and his family were living in the United Kingdom while Doug oversaw the company's UK operations.

I knew *Amway* was the oldest and most successful of all direct sales businesses and that DeVos and Van Andel were legends for what they built. I had already spoken live to hundreds of thousands of IBO's at *Amway* training conferences and had enjoyed the optimistic atmosphere at the events. I also learned that *Amway* stood squarely on principles of free enterprise and individual opportunity. I admired *Amway's* open advocacy of personal business ownership and it's unflinching support for the ideals of personal responsibility, hard work, delayed gratification and the honest production of wealth. These ideals touched a deep part of me that loved honor, honest effort and positive success. Because of this understanding of *Amway*, I was especially pleased to meet Doug DeVos. Here was a living representative of the free enterprise principles I had come to believe in.

Doug spent an unrushed two hours expressing his vision of a world where anyone could have the freedom to pursue their own adventures, paid for by an income stream they created by their own successful, self-owned business. He reinforced this with a natural, relaxed acknowledgment of God that further inspired me. He was a leader I began to trust. His heart won me. I believed he wanted to change the world for the good. I have since met other leaders who had the same heart, who wanted to change the world for the good. These are leaders who have built, not a support company like the DeVos and Van Andel families, but independent businesses of their own. I am forced by the reality of this form of communication to be selective. There are many others who deserve mention. But because of constraints, they are not included. Believe me…they are just as worthy as those mentioned here.

Jerry Meadows has always shown me the highest integrity. He and his wife Cherry have built their business to the level of triple diamond. Jerry was an engineer who moved to Charlotte, North Carolina with his young wife. They were approached by a new *Amway* IBO who sponsored them into the business. Cherry began to attend church with her new friends where she had an important spiritual awakening. Her husband soon followed her spiritually and together they began to develop their business. I once sat in a hotel room in Essen, Germany with Jerry and Cherry and listened as they told stories of their early days in the business. I still recall the emotional moment when Cherry said that she and Jerry had given their youth to their business. They believed in it that much! They now live in Franklin, Tennessee on an expansive horse farm, with white fences and manicured

The Amway Idea

lawns. Their children, Greg and Laura, along with their son-in-law and grandchildren are close. Their dream is now a reality.

I was first invited to speak at an *Amway* event in 1985. At the time I was assisting my friend Dr. Charles Stanley of the First Baptist church of Atlanta, Georgia. My sole responsibility was to speak whenever Dr. Stanley was away. Through a five-year association, I met hundreds of *Amway* IBO's who attended our services.

My wife Amy was captivated by the happy winning attitudes of these IBO's and soon began to buy and borrow as many audios of *Amway* speeches as she could find. We had a sound system that broadcast the speeches throughout our home and Amy would play the recordings from the time we woke up to the time we went to bed. I enjoyed the motivation and information, but began to tire of the non-stop flow. After Amy had obtained over 300 of these audios, I finally sat down one evening to ask her how long this was going to last.

Amy is sweet-spirited, positive and effervescent. She overflows with goodwill. She said nothing as I outlined reasons why we needed a break from *Amway*. When I finished, she calmly said that the people on the recordings were saying what she had hungered to hear all her adult life. She described her excitement on her 16th birthday when her parents gave her the one gift she asked for…a visit to New York City to hear Norman Vincent Peale. She remembered the moment when she met Dr. Peale. He gave her an autographed copy of his renowned bestseller, *The Power of Positive Thinking*. She then explained that the *Amway* speakers expressed the same exuberant optimism that attracted her to Peale when she was only 16. She noted the positive changes in my attitude as we had listened to the audios. She commented on how our preschool daughter Allison would lay aside her toys to listen to the presentations. She even asked Amy if we could be like these people all the time. Amy asked me to help her understand what these free-enterprise principles meant as she absorbed the information day after day. When she finished, all I could say was, "When do you think we can get more of these recordings? If they're doing all this for our family, we can't stop now."

Sometime after this, I was asked to speak at my first *Amway* conference. One of our close friends had just won the English Derby, and as a result, was presented to Queen Elizabeth II. Amy called her and asked what she should wear to the *Amway* event. Our friend Judy sent Amy the dress she had worn for the Queen with a note that said, "These are people who believe in success. You should wear this."

We drove to the venue in a motor home because we heard that many *Amway* leaders traveled in motor coaches. We usually used the motor home for church crusades.

When Amy and I were introduced to speak that evening, the crowd was wonderful. Applause roared and people cheered. I listened in amazement as the acclaim went on and on. I then turned to Amy and said, "Wow! This sounds just like the audios."

We did not realize that this would be the beginning of an extraordinary adventure. As of this writing, I have now spoken live to nearly 8,000,000 motivated people all over the world. Amy and I have made friendships that have nourished us for decades. Our children, Allison and Jonathan, are committed to free enterprise success for life. Allison, an attorney, credits the principles God blessed her with in the *Amway* business for the foundation of her career. Allison, because of the influence of *Amway* leaders, started her own business at age nine. She began to design and sell positive pencils with motivational slogans. She sold them to family, friends, IBO's at conventions and eventually to schools

The Amway Idea

and prisons. Her younger brother Jonathan bought the pencil business from his sister when he was eleven. It took him two years of effort and saving.

Allison used her pencil profits to help pay for college. She ended up graduating from Liberty University. She did so well on her LSAT exam, that she received a scholarship to attend The University of Kentucky School of Law. In law school she was elected to the student bar association, elected the co-president of the Christian Legal Society and elected the first woman president of the Kentucky Law School chapter of the Federalist Society (which she built into the largest chapter in the United States). She graduated from law school in 2008, passed the bar that same year in October and is now a practicing attorney.

Why is this important? Because she tells everyone that her accomplishments are firmly based on what she learned from the *Amway* business. This is one of the most meaningful examples of the power of the *Amway* ideal of freedom and success that I know.

Jonathan is building his pencil business as a teenager on the same success principles his sister learned. The same *Amway* leaders who inspired her are training him to build a dream and manage financial opportunity. This is living evidence of the life-changing effect of the American idea — *The Amway Idea* on every generation.

I have spent over 20 years observing *Amway*. It's not a perfect business, but I believe it's an excellent model for personal business ownership.

I thought it was important for you to know why I wrote this book. I believe individuals all over the world need workable opportunities for financial freedom that are backed up by honest, supportive people. I also believe that in a climate of economic confusion we urgently need clear expressions of free enterprise and positive capitalism. People need to know what works, what doesn't and why.

The Amyway Idea was written to answer those questions.

The Amway Idea

CHAPTER 6
Inspiration, Inc

Lights! Camera! Action!

There is something magical about a sizzling mass event. The excitement of history in the making! The joyous atmosphere of anticipation! The enormous crowds of people, coming together for a common purpose!

You have to experience it for yourself!

Political conventions have this emotion and power. Religious meetings share this surge of eager focus. Concerts and sports events have a strong entertainment edge that fans love and appreciate. This force of human desire and interest is also present at *Amway* conferences. The *Amway* meetings are often called "functions" because they have the function of training and motivating the thousands who attend.

Corporate business seminars have long had this element of inspiration. Wal-Mart is legendary for its pep-rally training style. Sam Walton, the founder of Wal-Mart, is still remembered for standing on chairs and leading employees and managers in Wal-Mart cheers. He would call out, "Give me a W" and the group would yell back "W!" He would continue until everyone had spelled out each letter and then call, "What does that spell?" The answer would thunder back "Wal-Mart!"

A student of Wal-Mart once wrote (in reference to their Saturday morning motivational meetings), "The corporation that loses out to Wal-Mart doesn't realize how crucial the Saturday mornings are to the success of Wal-Mart."

Wal-Mart, one of the most frugal companies in the world, still sends its managers for a week of training in the Wal-Mart culture each year. Well-known speakers, famous CEO's and high-level entertainers such as Garth Brooks and Donny Osmond are invited to teach and inspire. These events are theatrical, showy, fun and motivational. People who attend are encouraged to tell "SEE" stories. This stands for stories that communicate "Significant Emotional Moments."

All successful businesses provide motivation and training. It is the way they increase their odds for success. They don't offer training alone, because that could become dry and dull. Something has to get people's attention. They don't offer motivation alone because that could become emotionally shallow and quickly fade. It is the combination of both that creates the mixture of achievement. Training tells you what to do and motivation gives you the inspiration to do it.

Studies on skill development show that it requires 10 years to master a particular skill. It takes determination and dedication. A few years ago my daughter Allison and I traveled to Orlando, Florida for a golf clinic. We were taught by professionals who broke our game down and rebuilt it to be better. It was a rigorous and demanding experience. On the first day, we were filmed as we swung at golf balls. Then we were shown the film as a means to improving our swing. The entire process was filled with information as well as motivation. We listened to instructors who gave us pointers and encouragement. It was like a miniature *Amway* rally.

Regardless of what profession or career you choose, you will need help to get to the top.

The Amway Idea

Here are some great examples from different careers:

1. **Mechanic:** You will need to learn from someone who understands the details of machines and engines. A mechanic named Jim takes care of all my vehicles. He has spent 25 years mastering the intricacies of cars and their parts. I trust him because he has paid the price to become an expert.

2. **Medical Doctor:** The advanced education required to master a medical specialty is well-known. Anyone committed to this career must invest over a decade of their life to learn how to care for the rest of us.

3. **Engineer:** Would you trust the roads and bridges you travel on to someone who had not paid the price to learn all they could about structure and support? Aren't all those years of training worth all the effort?

4. **Teacher:** The children of any culture are critical to its future. Any society is only one generation away from barbarism. Teachers are the front line soldiers of civilization and must be trained to recognize and teach the truth.

5. **Professional Athlete:** Olympic scholars say it takes 3-5 years of intense development to give an athlete an opportunity to compete for minutes in an Olympic event. I was recently in a hotel with the New York Giants NFL team. I was impressed with their extraordinary size and their dedication to training. They pursued their own workouts and improvement programs, well into the night. They had been blessed with exceptional bodies and still realized the need to train their bodies and motivate their minds and emotions.

6. **Pastor:** A church pastor has an awesome responsibility for the spiritual welfare of the people who trust his leadership. In the Christian faith, of which I am a part, the emphasis is on the necessity of the pastor providing an accurate understanding of the life-principles of the Bible, as well as being an agent of comfort and moral guidance. This is why a pastor spends several years in professional training before he is given responsibility for the lives of other people.

I shared these examples to show that training, motivation and advanced skill development are vital to success in any field.

I want you to also appreciate that rallies for education and inspiration are common to all successful endeavors and are not unique to *Amway*.

Nordstrom, for example, has conducted "Recognition Meetings" for years. These events are filled with goofy skits, inspirational stories, "success pageants," cheers and fun contests. The company encourages monthly "MNS" competitions. MNS stands for "Make Nordstrom Special."

Nordstrom has four goals with these inspirational meetings:

1. **To show appreciation to employees for exceptional service.**
2. **To build team spirit.**
3. **To teach their people new ways to sell and interact with customers.**
4. **To perpetuate the unique culture of Nordstrom.**

All of these are done with open motivational flair and flavor.

Southwest Airlines publishes a "Luvlines" newsletter that

celebrates the milestones and achievements of its employees. A regular feature is a "learn from life" section that presents success stories from actual customer experiences. *Southwest Airlines* knows that their people need a regular dose of recognition and acknowledgement. They need to be noticed and appreciated.

Five things are common to Nordstrom, Southwest Airlines and all other super successful businesses:

1. **They all hold mass motivational meetings.**

2. **They all circulate positive books and helpful written materials. And they encourage their employees to study them.**

3. **They use audio and video recordings to increase the effectiveness of their training.**

4. **They implement coaching and mentoring programs conducted by people who have successfully done what they want their employees to do.**

5. **They utilize the best outside authorities.**

Amway leaders understand the principles of training and motivation. They know how crucial this level of education and inspiration is for those who dream of reaching their goals.

Behavioral scholar Frederick Hertzberg says that the five most important motivators for moving people forward are:

1. **Personal achievement**

2. **Recognition of that achievement**

3. **A sense of worth validated by your peers and based on your achievements**

4. **Increased responsibility because you've earned it**

5. The possibility of advancement without limit

Amway independent business owners are second to none when it comes to this level of training and motivation. When you build a business with this type of person, you build with the best.

I once did a study on the characteristics of the perfect personal business model. This is what I call a perfect POM which stands Personal Ownership Model.

I identified 15 traits of the perfect POM including:

1. Performance-rewarded. You earn what you get and get what you earn.

2. Independent. There is no requirement of a boss to control you or determine your options. You should be your own boss.

3. Home-based if you choose.

4. Flexible. You determine your schedule and how you will pursue opportunities.

5. Forgiving. There should be no penalty for delays and mistakes. If you make an honest error or don't do something in a certain amount of time, you can't be fired. It's your business.

6. Leveraged. You should be able to work with like-minded people who can help you succeed. You should not have to do everything alone. Your leverage should also extend to the opportunity to expand your business to and through other people.

7. "Brick and Mortar" free. Your business should not require a physical location adding expenses like rent,

The Amway Idea

utilities, property taxes and insurance.

8. Zero employees.

9. No formal education required.

10. No formal experience required.

11. World-class products and services.

12. World-class distribution channels.

13. World-class training.

14. Corporate support through product guarantees and reliable shipping and return policies.

15. Potential, legal tax benefits for owning and operating your own legitimate business.

You can see the benefits of this business model. It's for anyone who wants to own a business without the expense and demands of a conventional physical location store or franchise. *Amway* certainly fits this model. There is no better POM.

CHAPTER 7
Free to Be You

In the Bible (Genesis chapter 11), there is an unusual story. It is an account of an attempt by the human race to band together and build a structure "to the heavens." The structure was a tower and they named it Babel. God observed this action and decided to stop the project by confusing the languages of the different groups involved. Before this, everyone spoke one language. By confusing the languages, God would sabotage the venture. God's reason was simple. He saw that the people were working together for the purpose of dominating and controlling other people. Their selfish intentions motivated God to move against them. The story teaches that good and evil can both be multiplied by co-operative effort.

Some scholars have identified an additional lesson. The builders are using bricks for the first time in known history. These bricks are uniform – all alike. These scholars point out that God did not originally make bricks. He made stones and rocks which come in an almost endless variety of shapes and sizes. Bricks are the same shape by being forced into identical molds. Stones and rocks are distinct, individual and unpredictable. The idea is that God is more pleased with individual identity and development than a process where everyone is a copy of everyone else.

When a government becomes socialistic (in the Marxist economic sense), it operates through bureaucracies that exist to extend government control into private life. These bureaucracies seek to control more people by squeezing everyone into the mold the government has chosen for them. For this molding process

The Amway Idea

to work, individuals must increasingly surrender their personal goals and ambitions. This leads to the further surrender of personal freedoms. They must become bricks instead of unique stones and rocks.

The government in charge must do two things for this plan to succeed. It must control opportunity and result. When it controls opportunity it determines who is allowed to do what and restricts what you are paid for the development of your "opportunity." When it controls the result, it is telling its citizens how far they can go and how much of their own wealth they can keep. All this is done by extreme government oversight, including an over-detailed, smothering array of regulations. And of course, every government's favorite – ever higher taxes.

Always remember that the first step on this road is to convince people to accept their place as conformist bricks, not strong stones. This is usually done through fear. The government persuades people to believe that they are safer as bricks – that it will be easier for the government to take care of them if they are bricks. After all, bricks are easier to handle.

The problem with this approach is what you have to give up. You surrender your independence, your dignity and your chance to build your own future for yourself and your children.

It is my view that *Amway* has always encouraged people to reach for their own dreams to pursue their own chosen adventures. It has always invited people to be stones instead of bricks.

Benjamin Franklin famously urged the new American congress to select the turkey as the national bird of the young nation. His proposal was defeated and the solitary, majestic American bald eagle was picked instead. The eagle, with it's flashing eyes, fierce focus and mighty wingspread is a far better symbol of the dynamic American idea of free enterprise opportunity than the tasty, largely earth-bound turkey. The eagle with its ability to soar and command the air currents, is a fitting representation of the powerful energy released into a person's life when they really believe they can achieve their goals.

The back-bone of the *Amway* opportunity is this same American idea of personal freedom. *Amway* has always helped people become eagles.

This American idea is not the exclusive property of the United States, although the United States was founded on this belief. The American idea is universal. It exists for anyone who embraces it. This is the belief in the desire for "life, liberty and the pursuit of happiness" so famously stated in the American Declaration of Independence. This belief is expressed in the determination to throw off the chains of excessive government control, high taxation and the restrictions that come when a few officials decide what's best for the rest of us.

Millions of men and women have come to the United States to live this idea. Whether you are from Asia, Europe, Africa, South or Central America , the Pacific Rim or the rest of North America, you have a God-given desire to choose your own way. America is not just a physical location with borders and cities; it is a place of the heart, a dream of such conviction that men and women have gladly died for it.

Think for a moment about the eagle symbol. This great bird represents the spirit of free enterprise and the reward for honest effort embedded in the American idea. When you choose to pay a very real price for your own fulfillment of this ideal, you become an eagle. Your vision sharpens as you see what you truly want in life. Your wings spread as you soar to new heights. Your talons grip your chance for success.

The Amway Idea

Your *Amway* opportunity opens a door by offering you the chance to own and operate your own business. Only you can seize your moment. The parts are in place. They are just waiting for you to provide the spark through the unwavering commitment of your heart.

Bill Travis was a thief and liar. He abandoned a loyal wife and dependent children to escape his creditors. And he never returned for them. After wandering the American west, he finally arrived at a dusty, insignificant Texas village called San Antonio. While looking for work and food, he joined a group of Texas militia. Calling himself Colonel Travis, he eventually took command of the ragged group. When Mexican officials ordered the militia to leave, Travis and around 200 men refused to obey and barricaded themselves in an abandoned catholic mission called the Alamo. They had begun to believe in something bigger than their own lives. They had begun to believe in independence for what would become The Republic of Texas. A Mexican army under General Santa Anna surrounded the mission and demanded its surrender. Travis called all the men to a meeting in the central common square and gave them a choice to leave or fight and face certain death. The lone survivor of the Alamo told the story of what happened next. Tension lay heavy on the moment. No one moved. Travis drew a sword, bent forward and traced a line in the sand that would soon be wet with blood. Without a word he stepped over the line and turned and faced the men. One by one they began to cross the line until a flood of determined men came over to stand with Travis. They all came, moved by Travis' courage. They defended the fort to the last man. They all died for freedom, including Travis.

The question is, "What changed Bill Travis, a thief and liar, into Colonel William Travis, the martyred commander of the legendary defenders of the Alamo?" That answer will probably never be fully known. I think the main reason for the transformation of this man is that he came to believe in a cause higher than himself. He gave himself to that belief and it changed his life.

I know that it seems trivial to place your circumstances along side this man who died for his cause. However, remember this, you have a chance to seize an opportunity that could possibly change your financial future. You have a chance to do something to end the ceaseless pressure that ages you and your family. You have an opportunity to cross the line in the sand and change your future.

When the door opens to own your own business, you can use your eagle talons to seize the opportunity. Age, background, gender and color are all irrelevant. This is up to you.

In 1995 Joe Torre was 55 years old. His 17 year major-league baseball career was the longest duration for any player without a World Series championship. He managed three teams after his retirement as a player; the *New York Mets*, the *Atlanta Braves* and the *St. Louis Cardinals*. He was fired from all three teams and after the second dismissal from the *Atlanta Braves*, he was out of baseball for six years. He never won a postseason game as a manager. His win-loss record was 894 wins and 1003 losses.

Then to everyone's surprise, including Torre's, he was hired by the most famous team in American baseball history…*The New York Yankees*. The *New York Yankees* had fallen from their former greatness and decided to take a chance on Joe Torre.

The press conference that introduced the new manager was on November 2nd, 1995. The New York news media mocked and insulted the choice. Torre stood alone. The rest, as they say, is history. Under Joe Torre's leadership, the *New York Yankees* were great once again! They made the postseason playoffs 12 straight

The Amway Idea

years, won 6 American League titles and 4 World Series championships. The 1998 team won 125 games (an all-time record), as well as the World Series. Many students of baseball consider that team the best of the modern era.

Joe Torre saw his chance and grabbed it with the talons of an eagle. He was 55 years old and at the end of his career. He pushed for excellence and reached the top of his profession. Could your introduction to the *Amway Idea* be the opportunity you've been waiting for? It doesn't matter how old or young you are. It doesn't matter what you have already accomplished. All that matters is what you do now.

When I was in college I attended a lecture by a famous businessman named Colonel Harland Sanders – the founder of *Kentucky Fried Chicken*. He had been invited to speak on Christian business principles because of his deep faith combined with extraordinary success. When he finished speaking, I stayed to meet him. I was last in line. As I approached him, no one else was left in the auditorium. He was in his 80s and still lively and sharp. He shook my hand and spoke with me about the power of tenacity to make big dreams come true. He looked like a southern Santa Claus as he encouraged me to try going for something great. He closed with a mischievous smile and told me to remember that when he was 55 years old he had nothing but a dream and a recipe. He said he traveled to restaurants and even slept in his car to sell his chicken idea to whomever he could. According to Colonel Sanders, success came late for him, so I should learn to never give up. I could win if I just never quit.

I have seen people of all ages and types succeed in *Amway*. I met an 82-year old man (after I spoke at an event), who told me that *Amway* had revitalized his life. He thought he was finished. Now he had a list of new goals based on the growth of his business.

FREE TO BE YOU

I was eating dinner at Sallee T's restaurant in Monmouth Beach, New Jersey (my wife's hometown). Sallee T's is on the beautiful Shrewsbury River where it opens in to the Atlantic Ocean. I had just finished a crab dinner with Amy and her parents when a man stopped at our table. He said he wanted to thank me for helping him with his business. He had heard me at an *Amway* function and left determined to build a dream. His business had prospered and the income had given his family a new security.

I spoke to a couple in North Carolina who told me that their construction business had faltered, but their *Amway* business had sustained them.

I met a couple in Kiev, Ukraine who had traveled across 11 time zones to attend the *Amway* event where I was speaking. They spoke in awe of the fact that they could experience such an opportunity for themselves. They knew this was their great chance.

All of these individuals showed tenacity. I am from the Cumberland Mountains of Eastern Kentucky. I was taught early to value tenacity and long-term commitment. These would be vital to my success. These simple *Amway* IBO's demonstrated these qualities in abundance.

Jillian Strauss, a former program director for the *Oprah* show, recently commented on the results of her two-year study of the attitudes and perspectives of American men and women in their 20's and 30's (her own age demographic). She found a resistance to commitment that had detoured most of them from success and stability.

She described serial marriages as homes break up when partners become bored. She told of casual sexual "hookups" that leave people starved for caring relationships. She presented stories of couples living together with "escape clauses" in the back of their minds.

She considers all this an epidemic of selfishness. She writes that this failure of commitment pulls her generation down as they climb toward success.

A young woman told me that she was alarmed that her *Amway* business had not yet succeeded. She expressed doubt that the business model really worked. When I asked how long she had been in the business, she said, "Three months." This is the mentality of those who do not understand the principle of delayed gratification, as well as those who lack the tenacity to keep on going until they win.

Studies of human performance reveal that it takes 10 years of effort to master a subject or skill. The United States Chamber of Commerce estimates that it requires five years for the typical new business to "break even." And this woman wanted to quit after only 3 months!

We live in a hyper-accelerated culture. Speed rules. People are easily bored and easily give up.

What would happen if you countered this culture and grabbed this great opportunity? What would happen to your income and your future if you choose this business idea and simply never give up? Be an eagle and find out.

CHAPTER 8
Guilt-free Living

A few years ago I spoke at a summer family camp in New Jersey. Late one evening after the public session, Amy and I went for a walk. It was a balmy August night with a heavy scent of rose and honeysuckle in the air. We rounded a corner and saw a woman seated on a rustic bench beneath an arch enveloped with grape vines. She stood when she saw us and thanked me for my earlier presentation. We discussed the seminar for a few moments and then she asked if she could share something personal. My wife and I gave her our complete attention. She then stated that she was involved in something bad and needed to talk with someone. We all sat as she began her story. She said that she and her husband had three children aged 12 to 16, and had always hoped to build a family swimming pool for their kids to enjoy. They had worked hard and carefully managed their income. They had faithfully paid their bills and made regular contributions to their church. For five years they had saved money until now they had enough to build the pool for cash. She said that although the family goal had been met, she was filled with guilt. I asked why she was filled with guilt. She tearfully replied that she thought it was wrong to spend money on something as frivolous as a swimming pool.

I asked her several questions. Had she and her husband earned the money honestly? Yes. Had they met their financial obligations? Yes. Had they fulfilled their responsibility to support their church? Yes. Did they have a good motive and reason for providing the swimming pool? Yes…it was for their children to enjoy before they grew up and started their own lives. Then, I said,

The Amway Idea

what's the problem? I told her that she and her husband had lived quality, responsible lives, managed their money well and now wanted to give a reward for their labor to their much loved children. I said I was certain that God was pleased with them and wanted to bless their family. They had done nothing wrong. I then finished by encouraging her to enjoy every moment they spent in that refreshing pool. She came to her feet, her face radiant with a wide smile and hugged us both. She thanked us over and over. Her guilt was gone.

I recognize that this is an extreme example, but the story reveals some common questions when capitalism is discussed. Is it right to make money? Is it right to make a lot of money? Since this question often has religious roots, let me give a religion-based answer.

Western culture has a Judeo-Christian foundation. You cannot understand western civilization without a background in Judeo-Christian history. When Christianity began to take hold in the Roman Empire, it clashed not only with the dominant Roman society, but the Greek philosophical thought that underlay and informed much Roman thought. One strong element of Greek thinking was that spirit was always superior to the material. This meant that there was something suspicious about someone who openly pursued money. They were not spiritual enough. This led some early Christian thinkers to believe that money was tainted and unworthy as a goal. This contrasted sharply with Hebrew thought. The Hebrew's of the Old Testament scripture believed that although Jehovah was spirit, he had deliberately created a material world, filled that world with material pleasures and rewards, and pronounced it all good. They of course recognized that human sin, failure and selfishness had corrupted this environment, but the world God had made, was still something to be enjoyed. They believed that God gave material benefits to those who pleased and obeyed Him. Their own scripture says in Deuteronomy 8:18 that "It is God who gives you the power to produce wealth and so confirm His covenant."

The New Testament verse that causes the most controversy is the much quoted statement in 1Timothy 6:10. Most people think that the verse says that money is the root of all evil, but a careful reading of the original Greek text reveals that the accurate statement is that a love of money is a root of evil. Paul is writing here about particular people who were struggling with obedience to God. They were putting money before everything else. They were not condemned for having money but for loving money more than God. The warning is that this kind of obsessive, imbalanced love is an entry point to "all kinds of sin." The Bible never contradicts itself and there is no conflict between this New Testament statement and the numerous Bible passages that speak of wealth in positive terms.

Another objection to people producing large sums of money is that the economic resource pie is only so big, with a limited number of slices. And if you take more than one slice, you keep someone else from having theirs. This is a serious misunderstanding of capital creation. In a growing free enterprise system, your effort and investment produces new and larger pies. You make more, so you should enjoy more. A bigger pie also gives you more pie to share with causes you believe in.

Dexter Yager has built the largest *Amway* business in the world. I was with him once when a woman angrily challenged his decision to buy a new Mercedes for cash. She accused him of materialism and urged him to give the money away. Dexter was courteous and thanked her for her input. What the woman did not know was that Dexter had already given away more money than she made in 30 years and was using a small percentage of

The Amway Idea

his income to purchase a reward that he had earned. He owned companies that employed hundreds of people. His successful *Amway* business formed the foundation of years of generous giving. And I firmly believe that his personal rewards were morally legitimate. His Mercedes was a much smaller proportion of his resources than a $25,000 Chevrolet would be for someone making $50,000 a year.

The reason this is difficult for some people to accept is the widely-held but mistaken belief that when you make money you are morally required to give it away. Some people use an example from the life of Jesus Christ to confirm this. There is an account in the Gospels of a "rich young ruler" who wants to follow Jesus. Jesus tells him that he must first give away all his wealth and then he can become a follower. The young man "turns away in sorrow because he had great wealth." Jesus is targeting the young man's bondage to his wealth, not the wealth itself. Jesus correctly observes that the man's money meant more to him than anything else, and that this obsessive, imbalanced love of money stood in the way of further spiritual growth. The proof of this analysis is revealed when the young man walks away, having chosen his money over Jesus. Note also that Jesus never repeats this requirement to anyone else. If it were essential for everyone to do this, then Jesus would have told everyone to do the same.

This does not mean that you cannot give your money away. That is your decision. You earned it. The Bible says to give God 10% of your income in gratitude for his care and protection and to be generous in helping others. But it also speaks of the enjoyment of your rightly earned rewards.

I have one more important point. It is the wealth producers who create the jobs and opportunities for most other people. No one is helped when these entrepreneurs are penalized for their efforts. It is their drive and risk-taking that improve conditions for everyone else. Rich DeVos uses a simple formula to explain the genius of capitalism. He calls it MW=NR+HE X T. This is what the formula means when it is spelled out...

Material Welfare =
Natural Resources + Human Energy x Tools

His formula simply means that people benefit when our resources are energized by human effort, made more effective by the best tools available.

America was built by hard-working, risk-taking dreamers. You can still join their ranks.

CHAPTER 9
The Soul of Amway

I recently attended an event at the DeVos Center in Grand Rapids, Michigan. The hall was filled with eager men and women. I was standing backstage with my wife Amy and my son Jonathan. A roar erupted as the legendary *Amway* leaders Dexter and Birdie Yager sprinted to the podium. A four-minute greeting led Dexter to a special announcement. A speaker no one expected but everyone hoped for, was introduced. Surprise and pleasure filled the room as Rich DeVos strode on stage. Thousands of IBOs stood to express their appreciation and affection for the co-founder of the *Amway* opportunity.

I met Rich several times, and have always been impressed by his commitment to regular people. I once thanked him for his inspiration in my own life and he simply said, "All I do is tell people they can do it."

My wife, as well as my daughter Allison and I, once spent part of a day with Dr. James Dobson, founder of the influential organization, *Focus On The Family*. Dr. Dobson was a few minutes late, so we waited for him in his office. He walked in. Dr. Dobson was a big bear of a man. He apologized for keeping us waiting. He then grinned and said "You'll never guess where I've been. I just flew in from Israel on one of *Amway's* private jets." He went on to express his deep gratitude to Rich DeVos for helping him start the worldwide outreach of *Focus On The Family*. He recalled how Rich had encouraged him and financially supported him in the development of his ministry to families. He spoke of the wisdom Rich had always provided as a founding board member of *Focus On The Family*.

I still remember a conversation with a board member of the Robert Schuller ministry. He spoke candidly of the clear leadership principles that a fellow board member consistently provided. That board member was Rich DeVos.

This was the man I was preparing to listen to this special night in Grand Rapids. He began with a humble acknowledgement of the importance of the people who were standing throughout the auditorium. He told everyone that they, not he, were the reason the *Amway* business existed. He commended their courage and tenacity. He thanked them for their unwavering commitment to the American ideals of personal freedom and enterprise. He recognized their worth and appreciated their value. He meant every word and they knew it.

The peak of his presentation came when he told the story about how W. R. Grace Company attempted to buy *Amway* a number of years ago. Rich and his partner Jay Van Andel had no intention to sell, but were curious to find out what the other company thought *Amway* was worth. The two partners listened and received an offer that Rich called, "A really large amount of money." He never said how much the offer was for. Rich also shared how he had to explain to the W.R. Grace executives that he and Jay owned *Amway* but they did not own the *Amway* distributors. He also went on to tell them that they did not own the *Amway* belief system — *The Amway Idea*. He and Jay told the other men that they had misunderstood the concept. *Amway* was a way for any common individual to seize a dream and own their own business without the often prohibitive costs of conventional businesses. *Amway* was more about the human spirit than goods, services, buildings and products. When the meeting finished, Rich offered to sell an *Amway* start-up kit to Mr. Grace, the owner of the

The Amway Idea

other company. Mr. Grace declined and told Rich and Jay that he would now start a direct selling company to compete with *Amway*. He seemed certain that the two *Amway* partners had made their biggest mistake.

Mr. Grace did what he promised and a competitive company rolled out to take *Amway's* place.

Sometime later, Rich recalled being in a particular city and seeing Mr. Grace on the street. By this time the other direct selling business had failed and the Grace company had lost a considerable amount of money. Rich said he walked up to Mr. Grace and asked how his idea had worked out. Mr. Grace stopped and said, "You know d**n well what happened." Rich said he just smiled and said, "Well, I offered to sell you an *Amway* start-up kit!"

Rich finished this story to uproarious applause and then said what I believe captures the core essence of *The Amway Idea*. He said that Mr. Grace had failed to understand the one fundamental, irreplaceable ingredient in the success of the *Amway* business. At the heart of their business is the unshakeable belief in the right of the individual to build and own his own business. It is the universal need to be special, to protect and preserve one's personal dignity. It is and never has been a mere financial model. It is an idea that promotes a culture of success. It is the belief that the individual does not exist to serve a complex government system or to be swallowed by hopelessness and poverty. It is the belief that the greatest purpose of a successful business is to provide opportunities for further success, to the people it serves. *Amway* exists as a concrete expression of this basic human ideal.

It is obvious that many other conventional and non-conventional businesses are available to people today. It would be inaccurate to say that *Amway* is the only possible means of financial success. I do believe, however, that *Amway* has, from its beginnings, embodied the American ideals of freedom and personal opportunity in a way that has pioneered personal business ownership for anyone and everyone.

Rich ended his speech with a sincere statement of thanks to God. He is a committed Christian who never shows disrespect for the faith of someone else, and who also never fails to acknowledge the place of God's blessing in his own life.

As Rich walked off the stage he winked at me and said, "Hey Ball, how was that!?" He is a billionaire who did not need to speak to me. That's the kind of man he is, and that's the kind of business he represents.

CHAPTER 10
More Than Money

In October 2003, Amy and I were speaking in England at a large *Amway* convention. We shared the stage with a diamond level couple who had already become two of our favorites in the *Amway* world. Brett and Fran Deimler were among the youngest of all diamonds and a dynamic influence on everyone they encountered. Brett grew up in a large Mennonite-like family in Pennsylvania and Fran's family originally emigrated to the United States from Croatia. Brett saw the *Amway* marketing plan in his 20's and quickly built a substantial business.

I had always liked Brett for his exuberant personality and respected him for his unswerving honesty. Fran was tender, kind and beloved by whoever had met her. They both exhibited a warm and friendly relationship with Christ that influenced everything they did. They were an exceptional team who deeply believed in their *Amway* opportunity.

During the weekend, Fran seemed physically uncomfortable. She said she thought she had pulled a muscle because of a persistent pain in her back. We finished an excellent meeting and flew back to the United States with a promise to stay in contact.

The remainder of my fall schedule was followed by the Christmas holidays. I had continued to pray for Fran but did not consider the situation serious. The new year began with its usual excitement and potential. Sometime in the middle of January, Amy and I received a call from Fran. Because the pain had not left or diminished, she had an MRI exam on January 6. The report was a shock and concern. The test had revealed pancreatic cancer. The disease was already at stage five and her prognosis gave her no more than six months to live. Fran asked us to pray, not only for her, but for Brett and their children Angela and Anthony. Fran, being Fran, was more concerned for her family than herself. I still remember a comment she made at the close of the call. She wanted God to heal her. She also said that if God chose to take her to Heaven, she did not want anyone to blame God. It was just her time to go. This was typical of Fran.

For the next few months, she received radiation therapy and we all prayed. I then noticed something. Brett and Fran began to receive prayers and encouragement from thousands of *Amway* people around the world. Hundreds of *Amway* IBO's began to contact them and provide support. *Amway* friends took the children to school and prepared meals. Laundry and house cleaning was provided. Brett was able to devote himself to his wife as *Amway* distributors stepped in to give support. One *Amway* friend, Elaine Mallios, personally organized 40 women to give 24 hour a day assistance to Fran. These dedicated women, under Elaine's leadership, filled the gap for months. During all this time, Brett and I talked and prayed and prayed and talked. I would call Fran and try to lift her spirits and she would lift mine as well. *Amway* had brought all of us together. And it provided the social glue to hold all of us together.

As Fran weakened, she expressed her desire to live until her daughter Angela's 16th birthday. God granted that wish, and shortly after, Fran went to her heavenly home. The funeral was attended by almost 6000 people. It was the largest the community had ever witnessed. For six months, Brett and the children lacked nothing, as the flood of *Amway* support continued.

Fran prayed that Brett would be led to a great new wife who would love him and her children. God abundantly answered that

The Amway Idea

prayer. A few years later, Brett married Karen, a young woman of stellar character and impeccable quality. She embodies all that Fran believed in. She even loves Fran's children, as well as Brett. They met in the *Amway* business.

I recognize that this is a difficult story. You may be wondering why it is included in a book about success.

There is a simple reason.

The Amway Idea is not just about money – it's also about people.

Amway is organized around the "line of sponsorship." This "line" is made up of individuals who have established relationships with one another. It is a human value business. Nothing happens without personal contact and encouragement. Yes, *Amway's* focus is on the direct marketing of products. Regardless, everything is built on the relationships that provide flow of those products to the end users.

Triple diamond Cherry Meadows still tells stories of meeting her customers and distributors on Sunday night in an empty parking lot in Charlotte, North Carolina to fill their orders. One night they were surrounded by police who thought they had uncovered a drug ring. One of the policemen recognized Cherry as a member of his *Amway* upline. (This means the policeman is part of Cherry's downline.) Everyone laughed as they saw that the "drugs" were actually *Amway* soap products. Even the *"Amway"* policeman was in the fabric of *Amway* relationships.

When my grandmother Lafferty died, I was amazed by the outpouring of response I received from people I had met while speaking at *Amway* events. The funeral home director met me privately, and asked what he should do with the flowers and plants arriving hourly. He was already out of room. I have never forgotten the generosity of *Amway* people.

Once I stopped for the night at a lonely location in Pennsylvania. I had been traveling and speaking for several days and was unusually tired. It was a frigid January night and I took a walk around the property to unwind. I felt isolated and depressed. I circled to the back of the hotel and saw lights in a meeting hall. An event was in progress and people were outside for a break. I began to pass by when someone said my name. I turned and was immediately surrounded by dozens of *Amway* IBO's. It was a moment of mutual recognition. I had met most of these men and women at a larger *Amway* function. And now we are here together in a remote area in central Pennsylvania. The diamond who was speaking came out, saw me, and greeted me with a happy hug. It was a heartwarming experience.

Here are some other great stories that touched me…

I was checking out of a store at the *Epcot* resort in *Walt Disney World*. A young *Disney* employee looked up and thanked me for helping him with his life and success.

On another occasion, I was leaving Joe Victor's funeral in Ohio and waiting for a flight at the Cleveland airport. A woman walked up and thanked me for helping her with her *Amway* business.

I flew to Orlando, Florida and met my family at the *Disney Yacht and Beach Club Resort*. The Porter who carried my bags from the taxi turned and said, "The best life lessons I have ever learned, I learned in the *Amway* business. You spoke at a Sunday morning worship service following an *Amway* event and God changed my life. Thank you."

This one gets even better…

That same evening my family and I met friends for dinner at the

The Amway Idea

Mexican restaurant in *Epcot*. We were enjoying our food when the server came to the table with three other servers and a chef from the kitchen. He apologized for the interruption and said that they all wanted to thank me for the encouragement to do the *Amway* business. It was the greatest personal opportunity they had ever seen.

This is a business model based on your willingness to love and help other people.

Obviously not everyone lives up to this high ideal. All kinds of people sign up to do this business. There's always the possibility that someone will not have the best motivation. But as the examples of this chapter show, there are many others who base their business on respect for the other person. These are the individuals who honor the meaning of *The Amway Idea*. These are the ones who care. There certainly seem to be a lot of them.

This business idea works when relationships work. It is a people-to-people business. That is why it's called "direct marketing." In Malcolm Gladwell's bestselling book *The Tipping Point*, Gladwell says that there are moments when a "tipping point" turns the tide in a particular direction. He tells of how *Hush Puppie* shoes lost their popularity and the company that made them faced disaster. Without any apparent explanation, the shoes made a sudden comeback. No one knew why until it was discovered that in a certain city, a group of young trendsetters had chosen that shoe as their most "cool" accessory. This was the "tipping point" that brought back *Hush Puppies*. What matters here is that the shoe was saved. It was not saved because of a brilliant marketing campaign or a new sales strategy. The comeback happened because real people decided they liked the shoes and TOLD THEIR FRIENDS. They created the tipping point through a relationship connection. This is part of the genius of *The Amway Idea*.

People help people to help people who continue to help people. There are over 5 billion people in the world, and most of them need help to succeed. What better business model could there be to reach and care for so many people? There is truly an "idea" that can change the world.

It's called…

The Amway Idea!

The Amway Idea

CHAPTER 11
This Is Your Moment

Do you now see what's possible for you?

Consider the following story about what's possible when you embrace the moment...

In 1832, a British explorer was in the upper reaches of the Amazon River basin. He had been in the jungles of South America for months. It was wild, primitive and dangerous. He persisted because of a dominating goal. He had heard of a previously unknown species of small ostrich and was determined to locate this elusive bird. He hired local guides who helped him search, with no success. The creature either didn't exist or was too wary to be found. The effort was exhausting and after several weeks, he gave up and prepared to return to England. The night before his exit downriver, he sat down to a meal cooked by one of the hired guides. In the relaxation of evening, he slowly consumed the delicious bird on his camp plate. Suddenly, there was a flash of recognition and he realized that he was dining on the object of his goal. He was eating the reason for his difficult and expensive trip. He rose with a roar and began to collect the bones and other remains of the mysterious bird. He took the assembled body and returned to London where he presented it to the leaders of the scientific community. He was gratified when his find was recognized as an entirely new species. In his honor, the creature was named after him. The source of fame and wealth had been lying in front of him, and for a few frightening moments he didn't even know it. His meal became his monument.

Many of you have dreams of success and prosperity. You have

searched for opportunities that could change your life. What is wonderful is that your breakthrough may be sitting on the "plate" in front of you.

The *Amway Idea* has been in worldwide circulation for over 50 years. The beliefs and thinking behind it have influenced millions of people. There is nothing odd or mysterious about it. It is the classic *American Idea* of personal freedom, hard work, delayed gratification, a giving spirit, positive attitude and good, honest character. When people try to grab success without these basics, they crash and burn. There are reasons why America works. And to discard these reasons for a cheap, easy approach is to slam hard into the wall of history.

I told you in the beginning that this is an "essence" book. I hope you have drawn a key "essence" from every chapter. Each chapter gives you one insight into what gives *Amway* its remarkable character. Those insights can now be applied to you. What will you choose to do with what you now know?

I was speaking to 15,000 people at the Staples center in Los Angeles. I had spent an hour trying to communicate principles that would set them on fire and propel them toward success. I always pray before I speak, that God will help me help people. I paused at the conclusion, and instantly a simple thought exploded in my mind. I looked at this rocking crowd, and said that it didn't matter how much they had learned that night if it never translated into action. I waited a moment and then said aloud the thought that had burst into my mind. "Nothing is ever done until YOU do it."

This is dynamically true of you right now. Nothing will ever come true for you until you choose to act. Take what you have learned in this book and turn it into results. Don't wait. Don't debate. Now is your time.

The Amway Idea

If you live an "average" life span, the following holds true…

If you are 20 years old, you have already lived 7,300 days and you have approximately 18,250 days left. If you are 40 years old, you have already lived 14,600 days and have approximately 10,950 days left. If you are 60 years old, you have already lived 21,900 days and have approximately 3,650 days left. I tell you this as an inspiration. There is still time for you to have a great life. You just need to get going.

A few years ago my wife Amy, daughter Allison and I went to see a musical production of Jekyll and Hyde in New York City. The tenor who sang the dual role was exceptional.

The most thrilling scene came when Dr. Jekyll is preparing to drink the chemical solution that he hopes will free his nature from its tendency to evil and selfishness. Those of you familiar with the famous short story by Robert Louis Stevenson know that the formula fails and Dr. Jekyll transforms into the horrible and cruel Mr. Hyde instead.

Dr. Jekyll, in the play, looks at the glass containing his greatest dreams and sings the song "This is the Moment." This momentous moment is the hinge of the entire story.

Is this your moment? Are you ready to soar? Then take what you've learned in *The Amway Idea* and launch your life into the heights. Stop waiting for success to happen to you.

Make success happen for you by taking action and embracing *The Amway Idea* today.

ACKNOWLEDGEMENT

Thank you, Peter Wink.
You are a joy to work with and an excellent editor.
Cliche or not, I couldn't have done it without you.
— Ron

Go on a Honeymoon For Life!

Passion, Happiness, Satisfaction. Over 14,000 couples have experienced all this and more at *Honeymoon for Life*.

Do you want <u>the marriage of your dreams</u>? Are you looking for solutions for situations that have nagged you for years? Do you want the newest science on relationships that work? Then *Honeymoon for Life* is definitely for you.

This is not a seminar for bad marriages. It is a seminar for good marriages that choose to be great.

You will learn the secrets of an intimacy that reaches into your soul. You will discover working techniques that <u>fix arguments</u>. Together, you will both climb the *Ladder of Communication,* a unique program that teaches you to talk effectively about what really matters. You will experience fun moments as you laugh yourself to closeness. You will never forget the session on sizzling sex. You will <u>enjoy the hottest research on sexual satisfaction.</u>

Andrea from St. Louis wrote that her husband was an unromantic "clod." After the *Honeymoon for Life* weekend, she said that he completely changed. Months later he was still the "romance master" he became that weekend.

Bill and Susan (from New Jersey) had been happily married for 40 years. She wrote that the insights they gained in their weekend had transformed their relationship.

Michael wrote to say that he had not wanted to attend. He loved his wife, but hated the idea of a "gushy, embarrassing weekend." He went on to say that he was shocked at what a great time he had. It was nothing he had expected. He had super fun and fell even more in love with his wife. He added that sex was better than ever. He wanted to know when they could attend another one.

For information about the Ron Ball *Honeymoon for Life* marriage "excitement" seminars, contact Ron at 381 Maple Ave., Prestonsburg, KY 41653 or call Corky at 606-226-2294 or go to...

www.RonBall.com

Experience the Magic of Ron Ball Live!

Ron Ball has spoken live to OVER 8 million people around the world.

He has been the keynote speaker to 73,000 people in the Georgia Dome and taught small groups of success-hungry leaders.

Ron delivers information on fire. People change for good under his explosive impact.

Ron Ball is more than motivation. His seminars are loaded with usable techniques that get positive results today.

He has been compared to Malcolm Gladwell for his ability to surprise you into action.

Ron's popular topics include...

- **Linguistic Psychology**
- **The Amazing Power Of Your Words To Change Your Life**
- **How To Stand Out Like A Star**
- **21st Century Body Language Techniques**
- **What Your Relationships Reveal About You**
- **The Money Clinic: How Right Thinking About Money Can Make You Rich**
- **The Problem-Solver: A Point By Point Formula To Fix Your Problems**
- **The Brain Train: The Remarkable New Program That Can Change Your Life By Changing Your Brain**
- **The Amygdyla Secret: How The Emotion Center Of Your Brain Can Create Your Success**

This is just a small sample of Ron Ball's 200 acclaimed seminar topics.

To contact Ron to speak to your group call 606-226-2294 or e-mail him at *office@ron-ball.com*

Experience Ron Ball Seminars In the Comfort of Your Home or Car!

If you cannot make it to one of Ron's seminars…no worries!

Be inspired with Ron Ball's magical programs in the car, relaxing at home, in the shower or even while working out.

All of Ron Ball's seminars are available on CD including…

- **Linguistic Psychology**
- **The Amazing Power Of Your Words To Change Your Life**
- **How To Stand Out Like A Star**
- **21st Century Body Language Techniques**
- **What Your Relationships Reveal About You**
- **The Money Clinic: How Right Thinking About Money Can Make You Rich**
- **The Problem-Solver: A Point By Point Formula To Fix Your Problems**
- **The Brain Train: The Remarkable New Program That Can Change Your Life By Changing Your Brain**
- **The Amygdyla Secret: How The Emotion Center Of Your Brain Can Create Your Success**

To learn more about Ron Ball's CD programs, visit…

www.RonBall.com

Books by Ron Ball

Dawns with Dexter: *How Finding the Right Mentor Will Change Your Life Forever*

Ron Ball first met Dexter Yager in 1985. He was completing 5 years as a special assistant to Dr. Charles Stanley at the First Baptist Church of Atlanta, Georgia.

Dexter Yager was influential worldwide and enormously successful in the world of multi-level marketing.

Dawns with Dexter contains the story of how Dexter mentored Ron Ball using the same principles that transformed him from a struggling car salesman to a multi-millionaire businessman.

Worry No More! Proven Strategies for Parents

If you want to give your kids spiritual guidance that will make them like rocks in a turbulent world, then *Worry No More* is for you!" It offers timeless advice from well-known motivational speaker Ron Ball.

Order today at…